A new quarantine WiLL take My PlACE

APOSTROPHE BOOKS
P

Translations by Johannes Göransson:
Remainland: Selected Poems of Aase Berg
Ideals Clearance by Henry Parland

A NEW QUARANTINE WILL TAKE MY PLACE

¤

JOHANNES GÖRANSSON

APOSTROPHE BOOKS
apostrophebooks.org

Copyright © 2007
Apostrophe Books
All rights reserved

5 4 3 2 1

Printed in USA

Library of Congress Control Data

Göransson, Johannes.
A new quarantine will take my place / Johannes Göransson
ISBN 10: 0-9793627-1-7 (pbk.: alk. paper)
ISBN 13: 978-0-9793627-1-2 (pbk.: alk. paper)
1. Poetry
I. Title. II. Apostrophe Books (Series of 10)
Library of Congress Control Number: 2007939273

¤

barn | dödlighet infant mortality
- **fader** father of illegitimate child
- **föderska** woman in confinement

barnalstring procreation of children

barna | mord infanticide
- **mun** in the mouth of a child
- **mördare** infanticide

barnarbete child labour

THE SEMINAL UNION OF CARVERS

I've saved the best conspiracy theories for my own
   private genocide.
I've saved my own sweat for the trial, and the
   lingering doubts
for the lingering nights I spend in furious luxury.
I've saved my best thought for the last laugh of the
   century,
and my worst thought for the seconds after.
I've examined the bruise on your thigh and it looks
   nothing like your pet.

Beauty has become a riddle and the answer is grass.
Beauty was always a riddle, but now it's doused in
   gasoline.

I was born to break and break to be born again.
In my great novel the protagonist rides through the
   desert
searching for a lost father or gold.
It's a story of the death of narrative, the failure of
   history.
In my great debacle, all stories are starting to sound
   like Vietnam.
The enemies hide in bushes, the heroes go insane
   like helicopters.
I wrote the footnotes last night while the world was
   busy being victims.
It sounded more like a love poem than an explication
   of archaic usages.

It was the sickest excuse for love I've ever felt.
It was the second time I had ever been true.

The first time was when I joined the zealots
    plundering a home for the elderly.
The first time I was coping with Peace by
    pretending it was War.
Peace has made a farce out of my masculinity.
What will War do to me now that it's come at last?
What can I do with my devastation now that it has
    gone astray?
What can I do with my inmates now that the sheets
    tear every time,
now that the guards have grown jealous?

I'm stuttering into a phone. It doesn't work. It's not
    a phone.
I've come this far, almost all the way back to my
    master plan,
but I can't take another lie. My name has been
    written on raw meat.
The old ways were so glorious in all their savagery,
so full of potential that we never took time to abuse.

I've watched the river run itself ragged against the
    rocks
and I've told myself, That's not my army.
But it is, and the logging accidents pale in
    comparison to
the things that take place in my capital when
    everybody's looking.

I believe in military might and the military might
 believes in
my hocus-pocus . They've never seen such illustrious
 lies.
They've never felt such an illustrious hammer on
 their heads.
They've never heard such a laugh.
They think the truth is buried somewhere in
the backyard of my body. They think one shovel
 will do.

SHOTGUN WEDDING IN THE RIBCAGE OF THE BOURGEOISIE

This time around I'll be more obscure, more
unabashedly slashed in the backseat of the cab taking
me back to the barn where I've tied Shirley Temple
to a chair in an apparent homage to the tenderness of
the charlatan class. The thrill is gone. All that remains
are artistic movements and pig hoards trying to escape
from my room. The rain comes down like hammers on
infants. The parking lot stars know my story too well.
They are trying to pick up the broken bottles before
the immigrants come to exhibit their daughters in
white gowns and plastic tiaras. Their long and slender
fingers would be better suited to playing piano than
picking splinters out of little girls' hair.

Put out your tongue
here.
No, it's not an ashtray.
It used to be
but now it's my heart.

"Why do you always have to ruin your poems with
all this excess?" writes my former teacher who is
teaching herself to death in the soggy Northwest.
I'm just getting started photographing the pigs, using
the same rope as I used for the immigrant children.
Speaking of my damaged shell collection: My
infatuations are becoming increasingly militaristic.
Take Shirley. Just a few weeks ago I wouldn't have
taught her Spanish without first removing the duct
tape from her mouth. Take my torso. When I lived in
New York I would never have used scissors. I would

never have punctured the landscape painting without first painting the town with nail polish.

I must have fallen in love with an arms manufacturer's daughter.
She got me a job as a gravedigger in the Bronx.
I fled town when I found out that the children were alive.
I hid a fist full of Christmas ornaments in her back.

The new disease is called *Joy*.

Too bad I'm suffering from the old disease, *Barnslighet*, which is spread through publicly sanctioned arson and press conferences.

My rabble-rousing has made me into something I can't get rid of. Gratuitous martyr. Vivisection hallucination. Lawn fires would be the logical conclusion but it's not the 20th century anymore. The kill shelter is not my torso anymore, it's a Greek chorus investigating my bleep anatomies. They let a dog into my room.

It stares at me. Sniffs at my knees.
I can barely see its eyes glimmer in the dark.
It whines like Shirley.
It walks away.

Rock n' roll must be dead. The tsar is coming back and now he wants what's his. My train tracks are high on his list. And so are my clang ribs. You should be worried, dear figure skater. Your name has been crossed out.

Satie's soundtrack for *Parade* is the only piece of classical music I've ever passed out to. Listen. Can you hear the Hispanic children playing it with their sticky fingers? The same keys over and over. On the pigs' eyes.

Caricature exercise:
That's not a pig.
That's a celebrity
according to the World War II
documentary I watched last night.
You can learn how to cut
like this
when you're finished
with the immigrant children.
Here's a tiara.
Watch out for the rusty nails.
That doesn't come until later.

Come back to my strangle. I want everything we do to involve gibberish anatomies. That's how best to transform our teenage milieu into something less freezing in the basement. Your skin looks lovely and milky tonight, Hypothermia. Your youth looks like the fake state flower of this hyperbole. I could do such offensive wonders with your mouth, but I won't. Not yet. There are enough parasites in this bed to make me

royalty. King of Milk. Street of Thighs. I could make
such a wonderful cake out of your face.

We adapted Calvino's *Invisible Cities* because I could
hear a door slam shut.

My barn was built by a man who became famous for
his caricatures of military leaders. He drew generals
as pigs. He drew me as a punch in a model's mouth.
He made me a paradise of fat girls. It is a political
cartoon. I hang from the same gallows as Colin
Powell. And all the pigs wear smiling monkey faces.
I can't tell what the caption says. It's in German and
smudged with what looks like a crushed mosquito.
My caricaturist is gross. I'm full of puns and prickly
utensils. He learned his compositional elegance
from Dresden. He drew me as a roadblock. His
passport worked as an illustration of the well-adjusted
foreigner. My passport tells me to go home. I can't.
My land is over. I can hear the applause through the
wall.

The applause is dying down.
The audience is leaving.

I'm dancing with Shirley's ribbon in my mouth. My
race gestures offend animal rights activists. When the
flashlight breaks I use my own hands on the model.
She looks so much more colorful when I'm through
with her. Fine. Leave. Last night was far more collided
than this masturbation. Last night I was so far away I

OBSCENITY CAN
BE A FORM
OF ASCETICISM

couldn't cut the pigs, couldn't even put out cigarettes on my ankles. Last night sounded like burning books but I can still read the first page. It's about immigrant children. It compares their insides to the gray insides of crawfish.

OK, so I'm not a novelist.
The buzzards think I'm a propagandist for meat.
The giggly girls think I glorify insects.
The saints can't understand why the branches inside
   their clothes
break in the hours before dawn.

I'm eating pork tonight. I'm using it to bribe my model. I already gave her a camera. I gave it to her hard. I didn't do anything my brother didn't do to his apartment last night before blacking out. I wish he had saved the Replacements bootleg from Minneapolis, 1991. Since I went to that show, drunk on turpentine and laugh-track hysteria, fear has become my modus operandi. The hole in my head has become a salty flower.

The backlash has started to hurt the tourist industry.
My amnesia has made virginity self-referential.

There are plenty of prom queens to go around in this gymnasium but I want to make a brand new porno on this televised bombing of a chest. I'm starting to doubt the compositional elements of the epic. The witch-hunt metaphor doesn't work unless the reader

has experienced transcendence. The fish bait is rotting
in the swimming pool. The starvation exercises don't
work without bourbon. The charlatan class cannot
be burned without a more stupored mythology than
my barn. I need to improve the locks. I can't finish
the pigs. The countercreation has been co-opted by
adoption agencies. What should I do with the residue
on the balloon?

I need to paint my torso to look more like a torso and
less like a jailbreak.

I keep mentioning my torso because I wish I were a
zoologist. I wish I were a surgeon. Or Darwin. Or a
ballet impresario in Paris. Or a mole in the ground.
Or a reptile collector. Or 5000 accidents. Made of
swans. Or Darwin. Or an injury. Or going home in
a wheelbarrow. Or moving into the Hotel Fuck. Or
bleeding slowly into a silver bucket. Or plundering.
Most of all I wish I were Darwin.

Or 5000 accidents.

Made of swan feathers.

*Marco Polo to Kublai Kahn: My people will reduce
all these marvelous cities to sugar in a toothless
mouth.*
The Kahn: Are your people already that old?
Polo: No, we're infants. We speak in silhouettes.

OK, I speak in silhouettes and I do it with the zeal of
a marching band but I'm sweating profusely in the
sunshine and this plastic chair and my armpits and
my chicken neck. If there were some snow in here the
corridors wouldn't look so infected and the doctors
wouldn't looked so rubbed. The teenagers would stop
rubbing up against each other in the desks if someone
had the guts to throw a brick through the window.
There are no windows in this classroom unless
something has changed since I last opened my eyes.

      "Transcendence"

I use animals as props because they are made of meat.
I use the beautiful stars of track and field because they
    won't
make it through the desert. I'm using this house
because it's not mine. I'm imitating a divorce between
    the head
and the heart of a dissected eagle. I'm the son of a liar.
A fortunate son. My fortune is a burning barn.
My fortune says: Go home, burning child. I was born
on the border. On the other side: daguerreotype,
    winter.

(I erased the final paragraph because I don't want to
be fired and I don't want Ashcroft to throw me out
of the country. He cares so much about the youth of
America, he would never stand the neighing in my
barn. That fucking pervert loves to drink milk in the
dark. I should know. I made him. Nobody grows up

in this torso. Nobody can act with duct-tape over their mouth like our starlet can. The final scene: trapped animals. Scratch. Scratch.)

RETINA, IGNITE

There are many reasons why my reconstructions
fail. For one, horse screams are impossible outside
elevators. We need grates. We need some space to
bleed. There are many titter-tatters inside God. There
are many feet kicking. There are many reasons to want
out. My hares are offensive. Listen to them digging in
the sand. Listen to my squandered chest. Listen.

The birds of paradise have expired.

They must have been throbbing. They must have been
bright. Touch. There are many reasons we feed them
to the pigs. They don't make any noise in the pigs'
mouths. They flap but they cannot make any more
sounds. The only sound in this museum: a centipede
burrowing into your eardrum.

Listen. The funeral has begun.

The Sound:
kneeling, incised
barked torso
ornamental infanticides in the ceiling
soak a foot in salt water

If the marching band is tearing down the cutout
Christs, who is painting a bird on my chest? *That
plucked anatomy doesn't look like last night at all.*
That's a joke I keep telling myself about last night to
confuse the gentle peruser who wants to stab open my
landscape painting to feel the stained hares inside. She

wants to knead them like dough in my hands. When
I talk about last night this openly, I am joking in a
panicky way. When I say "last night," I don't mean
night as much as a woman, the white color of her
thighs. Or the swan that burst out of my wife's dress.
Or my wife's voice in my ear. Or my flocked torso.
My barked torso. My car alarm car alarm car alarm.

Iconoclastic Riot:
traversed
distance

After puncturing the grand opera,
we moved into more advanced anatomies,
teaching immigrants how to speak
with peanuts in their mouths
while watching the tiger devour another lamb.
Now all we have to do is teach them
how to find a tunnel and douse it.
We will be stuck on the other side.

Last night's architecture exhibits many foreign
influences. The ceiling is unusually low for a horse
show. Walls are not usually this thick unless the
rooms are used for interrogations. The main stylistic
impulses of the decorative patterns seem to come from
the orient or some such illusion of tranquility. The
persistent iconographic feature of the open eyes seems
to come from the fire. The realistic style is nostalgic.
The flecks on the torso appear to be real blood, if not
human blood then the blood of a horse. The birds

REVULSION AS AN ANTIDOTE TO EXPERIMENTAL POETRY

are trying to escape. The glass is almost unbreakable
unless you use a hammer.

The poem engraved on the torso should not be read.
Its obscene depiction gives us an idea
of what the architecture looked liked before the fire.

No pigs in the elevators! No pigs in the women!
No disfigured birds or pigs or horse screams! And
absolutely no drive-in theatrics with my x-rays!

I'm reconstructing the horse farce with a garden hose
    and an infant.
The only problem is that all these beautiful birds
disfigured and fed to grunting pigs cannot fit into the
    elevators.
I want to fit them all into the eye of a needle.
I want to stitch up the landscape. I want to drive the
    bungled
innocents down the well and into town like loud
    lambs.

        Come my chosen birds
        Come my brick narrative

The theme of the futility of reconstruction is inscribed
in my medicine chest. I'm scratching through the
shelves searching for a drug to swallow, the right
implements to make a cut.

When I tell you that I'm trying to reconstruct last

night's architecture I mean that I'm trying to drown
a horse in a mudslide or a kindergarten. When I tell
you that God is violent in the elevator I mean: there
is not enough space for all of those hammers in your
seashell collection. A torso can contain an entire
October of birds. But eyes can only take so many
breakouts.

    A torso can contain a travesty of stitches.

What do you keep inside your abandoned factory?
I keep carving up my legs up there in your abandoned
    factory.
I keep pearls soft in my mouth. I keep my hares hid in
    my woman.
I clean a woman with turpentine. The hares will be
    safe in there
but they will choke, choke wonderfully like a car
    alarm.

I've been worried about my slippery puzzle since I sat
through a movie about traffic jams hiding my hares
inside my shirt. I thought they had sharp teeth but they
don't have any teeth at all. They don't even have a
mouth.

Bleed my hares. Bleed me a bed for all the starving
children. Bail me out. Not because I'm innocent but
because the show must go on, and the show needs a
pair of eyes that have been used for photographs. This
is not my voice. It's a recording.

The hares are breeding in the cabinet. This is my voice. This is my Rome raised for the barbarians. This anatomy was made to model for Dührer's allegorical representation of corruption.

Green. That was the color of my eyes when I wrote a poem called "The Diary of a Pig Circus" about the assassination of my silhouette. I will probably paint over the naked girl with the guitar string because I like to keep my music clean and my girls alive. The mice scurrying around in the projector sound like an itch. The kneeling figure with his arms outstretched is the donor. His body is drawn with great plasticity, a style that was later eliminated by the linear styles of the later period.

We need some space to bleed.
We need a tree in which to breed.

(Why is the bird still intact?)

"In general the picture is the apparition
of an appearance." (Duchamp)

This command was written on a mural featuring children rising out of boxes. The style suggests a direct influence from the international Gothic workshops. The snakes are undulating wonderfully in the pajamas. The holes are in the bellies. I'm writing this poem on a cutting room floor while editing a documentary about the Massacre of the

RONALD REAGAN BROUGHT ME TO THIS COUNTRY – ME AND THE ANTI-ABORTION MOVEMENT

Innocents. Before I came in here someone was editing
a film about distance. The landscape is shot from far
away, from behind a wall. The soldiers are curious.
The working title is "Ostranenie." The voice-over
is Shklovsky reading *Zoo: Letters Not About Love*.
Berlin looks laughable with all those mothers wearing
fur.

My hare is shivering here. Touch me. Here. Here.
"Am I really that disgusting" shouts one of the
strippers into my ear. "No, I'm cold" I shout back
but I keep looking at the scar on her little belly.
The gorgeous money shot will be dismantled on the
sidewalk. The scar will be erased.

Do you want my broken fist? It's actually my brother's
broken fist but he won't need any broken fists in the
barn where he's going to sell pearls to swine. He's
going to engineer a change. I hope to engineer my
emptiness into another kind of animal, one less likely
to get struck on a dark highway. The final paradigm
of the landscape as a reclining woman would be
pacifying if it weren't for the smell of oven-gas and
the holes in my eyes.

I can't see a single thing
I don't want to wear
on my body like a car
skidding out of control.

I joined the Big Dance with a rotten scarf wrapped

around my baby sister and a theological look in my eyes. I originally ended this with a shiver in the animal and an image of distance as salvation. I'm discussing the recreation again. Realizing that it will fail again. My torso was not made for birds. It was made for herds and Rome and I'm erasing my vocabulary of dispossession. If I had my choice, I wouldn't even be here. I would be painting an odalisque with wonderful slabs of thighs and a choke collar that would be too tight around my dog's throat. My dog's dead and buried in a cornfield in Iowa. Listen. No.

"SELLOUT JACKET"
(ROYAL ALBERT HALL)

My rage has a white face.
It looks like the white face of colonialism
but my natives eat the horses at night.
My natives fuck like a bag of spiders.
My girlfriend is gasping for air; she's going catatonic
in this bargain bin of a winter, she's scared of pigeons.
I own a shoddy collection of pigeon skeletons.
I never thought I would be able to fit so many
disparate parts in my mouth at once.
I have gone sour, gone to gashes,
gone to find the missing pieces to my hysterical
collection of used razorblades.
I collected hands in Italy but the plaster
was too delicate for my hammers.
I picked cockroaches out of a famous haircut
while a fat lady screamed in my ears.
My collection of fevers is the loudest
this side of the 19th century.
My car has run out of gas.
I have split all the souvenirs from the empire
into opposites – you and then, her and now,
black and simple, lipstick and extinction.
They're in the trunk. The natives will steal them all.
But by the time they come here to stick their
fingers in my engine, I'll be long gone
hauling my mechanical masterpiece through
the woods as if I were salvaging a child from a fire.
I'm saving a childhood that is burning down
like bed sheets. I'm breaking up its bones.
They look like pigeon bones but there are no wings.
There are no eyes to look at me.

WE WILL USE
CLOTHES-HANGERS
NEXT TIME

Today my kaddish class is learning slapstick. Pigs are slick. Sharks are easier to cut with one's eyes taped shut. Even the most vandalized student should be able to find the ribs. Even the most benign student should be able to rearrange the token organs (rope, photographs, wasps, dance shoes) on the steel table. Even though their eyes compare favorably to my own in certain lights and freezing landscapes, pigs will not be used in this year's prom coronation.

The crown will be less fetal this year, less slurred. The pharmaceuticals won't look like shells. We will clean the parking lot with a riot hose. Even with scabs, the lamb will be perfect for the parade. Every miscarriage must be pieced back together if we are ever to prove the hardcore value of non-representational art. We must run out of the abortion clinic before the smell of kerosene saturates our vestiges. We must get the popcorn out of our teeth. Watch symbolists do their thing with rabies.

The look of the ribs in their quick hands is so modern.
The look of their mothers is so cockroached.
Their fathers are out in the fields dancing with locusts
    in their music.
In court their children are complete.

The subject matter of this class is as obvious as a butchered pig, as cut up as the wedding I ran into last night with a sharp object. If you can't figure out what I'm talking about, you filthy girls have no right to call

THIS SILENCE
WOULD BE MORE
PEDAGOGICAL IN A
MEATPACKING PLANT

yourself strippers. Hint: It's not the same object I used in the concussion. It's the only thing I saved from the wilding. It may be an oriental instrument. It's stringy. It may be my arms. It must certainly be broken before I hand it back to the slumlord.

Here. Pass it around.

Next unit: Colonialism. Well, well, well! Look who's here for our drive-by exercise in innocence. Where were you last night? Did you see the bride mistake me for a distance? Did I look explicit with the plastic bag over my head? Next unit: Deportation.

We're marching toward a grand exposure.

Keep the lights off! No totalizing narratives! X-ray the horses. Map out my migration patterns with hammers. Heat the ovens for the picture show. Remove your barbwire, your blackface. Tear the heads off tin soldiers. Pass them around.

Tell the slumlord I'm lost.

Next unit. This is Los Angeles of Fire and Looting. The bull has been cut open and redecorated with reams of white pages. Make your diary out of the blotches. Build a cage. If you're a cheerleader, don't forget the vermin in your outfits. If there's no end in sight, wipe the blood off the muzzle.

Today my insect class will theorize about the locust nature of translation and how this physical activity pertains to the language of miscarriages. Today a sage will tell me that I cannot write in a language my mother didn't speak when I was rattling in her womb. He'll tell me that my locusts are just another form of masculine self-hatred, that my convulsionary lacks the bones necessary to indict our culture on charges of cakewalking on infants.

Tomorrow you'll have to go back to the language you were born to speak, crayfish. That's what the sage tells me while poking my students' mouths with something that looks like a bicycle pump.

You writhe like you were trying to shatter a doll's head or apply make-up with termites on my arms.

This is how I speak dirty.

That's what I tell my students when they ask why I won't play backyard with them. Maybe some day I'll be reincarnated as a strip mall or a book-burning. This song used to be an equestrian silence. That's what I told you at the meatpacking plant.

Next unit: free will.
Next unit: prison reform.

My students are stuffing my head with used balloons.

I remember every single one of those balloons.

How they broke and smeared how my sweetheart's
belly glistened how I picked hair out of my mouth.
Today: I will recite satires about crowd manipulation.
You will draw the rashes on your thighs, the trashed
placards that were my chest. Today we will study
medical allegories and breathe numb as stampedes.

Next unit: Pedagogy.

Modernity can look so shockingly bright, so
shockingly like ribs from the point of view of
someone carrying a contrived pig through the now-
now-now of adolescence. It should have been less
narrative, but I wasn't the one who drew up the plans
for the robbery. Next unit: jingoism.

Blind students, forgive the deaf students
for what they did
to your craniums and shoulder blades.

In case your babies are worn out, we have a laugh
track, I shout above the helicopter noise. In case your
eyes are worn out, that's crinkled newspaper I'm
stuffing my students' heads with. Stuffing their bodies
with feathers from a nearly extinct bird. No, that's a
bird.

Tomorrow: Geometry, the mascot of our collapse.

Final Exam:

If you see a flower you will make it out of here. If you

MY MAKEUP HASN'T
EVEN DRIED YET
AND I'VE ALREADY
WRITTEN A POEM
ABOUT EXPERIENCE

see my daughter ask her where it hurts. If you see a
factory you should go into child psychology. If I'm
wearing a plastic bag over my head wait until the dog
gets hit. If you're already smashing windows flinch
for the camera.

(Turn on the radio with your clean hand. The crackling
is the sound of our cakewalk. We're learning how to
speak again, Herr Sage.)

Today we're finishing the school, Herr Sage. The
dean is hammering in the nails. My nude arms have
goose skin. My students won't let me bring the rabbit
parts into the elementary school. The guards won't
let me back across the border. The tracks are so soft
in here I can almost feel my way into your field-trip
symbolism. I can almost hear the locusts in my own
chest without puncturing the canvas with my only
silver fork.

My students have stopped speaking. The dean has
stopped breathing. My maps taste like chewing
gum. I must be in my bedroom again with my eating
disorders. I'm trying to chew up the distances that
throb in my body. I'm trying to eat cake until I puke.

I yell to my students: Fellow tourists, this is how you
hold a hammer in the crumble. This is where I leave
you to find your own way out of the Laundromat. The
final is a riddle. Hint: The border patrols speak my
native language, doors slam in the neighbors' house.

TWO POEMS ABOUT HYGIENE

1.
I think therefore I am a barn none of the animals
 escape from.
I think I am an arsonist, therefore I am.
I think I soaked the chicken in gasoline. I think I stole
 that idea
from a Medieval representation of the Bubonic
 Plague.
I stole my persona from a rabble with raised fists.
My mask is starting to wear out my nights, starting to
 feel
like a nest of wasps, to look like my face.
I mean the ratty face I've been wearing since I moved
 into
my brother's living room. I moved in here because
 I'm running out
of money, running out of clues, running out of an
 exhibit
of postcards from my hometown.
The exhibit is a study of the vermin that infested our
 lives.
I was too young to remember.
My only knowledge of vermin comes from a lame
 puppet show
about the Spanish Inquisition I witnessed one day in
 the park.
The enraged children rushed the stage and tore the
 whole thing
to shreds. I passed the ordeal while walking to class.
In those days, I was studying the law, thinking it
 would help me

silence the barn. Help me finally incinerate the
   animals,
make necklaces out of horses' teeth.
Then I became a painter of sentimental landscapes.
Then I became a choir preaching to my executioners'
   children.
Don't take my word for it.
Touch my lips with your favorite piece of dirty broken
   glass.

2.
The so-called experts all claim I've filched my vision
of New Jerusalem from an abortion clinic,
but those experts have never even tickled an infant
with a knitting needle. They don't know how hungry
 I am
or why my Jerusalem seems fragile as a ribcage.
They plagiarized their theory from an obscene letter
 my insane
ex-girlfriend wrote to the local newspaper during the
 period
which became known as my personal Diaspora.
Maybe you've heard of my scotch-guard Damascus?
I only learned three things from those years:
If you want to get rid of a baby, throw out the bath
 water.
If you want to get rid of a shivering lamb, toss it into a
 room full
of starving dogs. If you want to get rid of me, you're
 out of luck.
I've tried my whole life. We must be twins.
We must also be lingering imagery from the Cold War.
We must be a cold war, a cold and clammy little war
we won't win until one of us is deflated in the
 tabloids.
But neither one of us is the kind of person to get
sentimental about putting out cigarettes on our arms.
We were born with pigeons flapping in our mouths
and a barn full of reckless animals struggling to
 escape.
They want to come out to play. They want to disrupt

the hastily assembled rehearsal for my shotgun
   wedding.
They know if I marry my girlfriend, I will stop.
My girlfriend doesn't acknowledge the animals
and thinks you are a thief locked in a vault. She's a
   scientist.
I'm a science full of scalpels. I'll leave you to the
   burning.

AUTOBIOGRAPHY

You can't teach Fame new tricks.
It won't come when called, it won't drink anti-freeze.
How do I know, my lovely disorder?
I tried to escape from words to shine.
I traveled on the back of a teenage beauty queen.
We barely made it out of town.
The wilderness was lackluster and the extension
cord wore thin. Her lips smeared.
I climbed out of the debunked allegory
and walked back to my screwdriver.

By now you're probably rolling your eyes. By now you
probably think I should have outgrown the role of
backfired king in a farce that still feels shockingly
    alive to me,
despite the fact that it has been canceled, despite the fact
that the orchestra should quit playing sterile out of tune,
should stop using their accordion to trap mice in their pit,
should stop representing Europe as a relic from
concentration camps and cabarets.

*

When I was little, my parents gave me a gun to keep
me from crying. It wasn't loaded but I tried. I've
grown up with it. I have invented more functions for
it than its inventor could possibly have imagined,
unless a woman stroked his hair; unless he felt like a
raided warehouse; unless Death was rehearsing in his
bathroom, wearing your jewelry and your make-up.

Oh, so *you're* in this poem now?
You with your fingers and curls and
the mayhem you confuse with intimacy.
If it's a ghost town you want out of life,
find a man made of feathers
or a saint from The Great Polio Epidemic.
If it's a siege you want, find religion in a shoe box,
then throw it back in its hole.

I'm in another business entirely.
My store is a parking lot in Duluth, MN: 3 a.m.,
    streetlights.
My favorite product is tarnished by translation.
My favorite phrase is a knock-off from the insurrection.
My favorite ad is a swimming pool in a pasture.

Will you be my Valentine?
It's a little like a coloring book for children with
attention deficit disorder, a little
like running a civil war into the ground.

*

My gun and I are the only ones keeping the family
    traditions alive,
lying here lying to each other about my crooked
testicle and the origin of the word *infested*. No, that's
not all we talk about but that's all I'll tell you. This
isn't a confessional poem. This is a family

history. My family is over. Your family is a garish game of hammer-and-nails. You're the daughter of a million loose screws and I'm the son of the century. Unfortunately, the last century. Unfortunately, I was disowned. Unfortunately you're teaching me your neigh mythology with my mouth. Together we make a glamorous couple and a candid conceit. Together we make a fancy misreading of the pigeons shitting in the branches outside my window. (You think they are doves, that they represent Peace, I think they represent my bogus heart.). Together is a place I can't understand, no matter how many construction companies I hire to represent it with wrecking balls.

*

Things to do:
- check the burners
- buy a pound of ground meat
- check the showers
- tell the landlord he's a cheap pig
- tell the landlord he's a tool in the meaningless
    workshop of capitalism
- paint the walls
- tell the landlord what I'm going to do with him when
    the revolution comes
- check the burners
- buy a pound of ground meat
- take a shower
- take a shower
- check the burners

I whisper to Fascism and Fascism whispers back to
me like a choir of quivering girls. Most innocence
has been filched. Most innocence is the innocence
of infanticide. Most visions of joy are metaphors
for death (the varnished child, chartered lawns, the
oblivion cement, the suit that fits perfectly when
you're lying perfectly still). Once I picked up my
kitchen knife and played with it in a dangerous and
pathetically dramatic way. Actually it was just before
I wrote that sentence, maybe ten seconds ago. (But ten
seconds is a lifetime for some animals.). My gun is
jealous of the knife because the knife actually exists,
the way my fingers exist when they touch your belly,
and because I'm talking to you and I haven't talked to
my gun for at least a week. I've barely even touched
it. I've touched it as if it contained asbestos. I've spent
my nights reading my favorite book instead. It's a list
of words. It has many bite-marks from a dog that was
killed by a mini-van. It's a book about God but it's the
bite-marks that I love.

Another way to express this insight
is to say something witty in a foreign language
while polishing my dad's old razor blade.

I bet by now you're wondering what happened to the
teenage queen from the first part of this poem. Or have
you forgotten about her bruised hips and nonchalant
way of chewing gum, her odd way of twitching, her
love of the fist? I took her to a repair shop but the
owner was gone and his eyes were closed. I took her

to the infidels but so did a hundred other perverts. Let me tell you what I finally did, what finally earned me a spot in our obstinate pantheon - I lured her into a cake and told her to not jump out until I say "The End." The End. She's not listening to what I say anymore. She's cold in there. She's in there with the other characters from this exhaust pipe of a disco. It's been ages since I saddled her conscience with my bitter pill. She swallowed slowly, she graced my chest with her lips. The End. She committed a crucial mistake. She believed I was a sign from the heart of her story. She wanted to reach the end. The End. She wanted to be a child with a child, a house with a pool, a perfectly laundered load on a shelf, a book with a beautiful spine. The End. Most games end when the children go home. Most empires collapse into incest. Most suspicions are valid. Most songs fade out. How do I know this? I've been sitting next to this damned radio long enough to have channeled every voice through my skull-bone. I sit in a field fledged with plastic wrappers and paper shreds. The radio has no cord or the cord is a snake. The snake is a tire. I'm tired of words. The End. She's shivering in there, in the cold cake, practicing her lines. She thinks it will be a play. It won't. The End. I'm going in. The End.

PIG CIRCUS

Sometimes there is a beautiful world inside the world of poetry. Sometimes the children have nosebleed inside my ornithologies and sometimes the cheerleaders are naked inside interrogations I keep holding to prevent myself from defacing all the posters you've pasted up around my room. They inform an anxious public that there is no place for a crowded elevator like me in an age of retrospectives and beautiful poetry about the origins of deficient landscapes.

I want to dig my own ditch in that landscape.
I want to bury you in that ditch. I want to bury
the hatchet in the back of my poem, in your back,
I want the sheets to depict men with nothing
left to bury. Such men don't deserve to lie on glass.

Sometimes we leave my body inside the allegory and sometimes there are still traces of the beach on it when we get to church. Sometimes we leave the taxidermy museums with new concepts of liberation and defiance. Sometimes the rewards of poetry are like the lessons of the Native American exhibit on the third floor:

        Pale, decorative, slow and glorious.

Sometimes I wish it were men in there.

I want to learn how to touch you
like extinct animals.

So far, I've only got the panting right.
My hands still scratch too hard
still hit hard still stroke like
an animal that won't die until
the bank of America has been depleted
of all of its beautiful secretaries.

Oh, beautiful secretaries at the Bank of America!
Meet me tonight in the taxidermy museum of your
    choice
and we'll stuff the animals full,
as full as the collapsed bunker
where I built a glass bed for my girl, where I painted
the walls with fluids left over from our lovely theater
of arguments and spilled milk .
Those fluids tasted oddly like bourbon and oddly
like the aftertaste of fame.

I'm never going back to the Bahamas.

I live in a corrupted landscape: The fruits have no
flavor. The girls have no odor. The boys cannot break.
Their language is Latinate and there are no words
for hyena or thigh. I can't say anything without my
hands and my damned hands will only hit or strike or
beat. I have been offered the job of explaining U.S.
involvement in the Third World using a puppet theater.
I told the fiction writer in charge that I knew nothing
about the Death Squads or disappearances. "Just think
about the way I held you last night," she said and
smiled the smile of a thousand cigarette burns.

Stockholm Syndrome is the perfect disease for me.

(A transcription of my roommate's recordings, heard through several walls and a few rooms:)

Don't ask me.
Unless you want to wear barbwire on you're child's
 ankles.
Unless you want to listen to music while tied to hares.
Don't ask me to shoot the tigers.
Don't ask me to explain asylum laws.
Don't ask me about Bosnia.
I'm sick as the crystal nights in which we made
love like horses in a mudslide.

Blackout

I've never wanted to meet God.
I don't like any other children
than my sweet little pet theory
about displacement.

The codfish is wrangling.

Will I take you to the skinny house or to the famines
I've fabricated while trying to figure out where to
take you, where I can position myself so that I won't

escape so that we won't escape so that we won't break
the glass before we've finished the new house.

The one that doesn't end.
The one with the blue flowers
I planted on your thighs.

Yes, that one. Yes, the pig circus. Yes, in half. Yes,
every hole. Yes, ivory. Yes, bright. Yes, nothing. Yes,
that's gasoline. No, that's a torso.

Our Lady of the Pig Circus
The First Cut of Our Pig
The Piggie Bank, Piggie Bank

There's no place for you in the beautiful world of
poetry. Not with all these alarming connotations of
child molestation. Not with your absolute lack of
symbolism. I want to keep you in my room. I want to
tie you up like a deer.

Elsie,
We made cuckoo love
it was cuckoo love
it was trauma to the chest
it was knock-knock-who's-there
it was a cuckoo clock in the breakneck
harpsichord thumping against
my seal. My seal is so soft,

so soft, Elsie. Its babies have been
clubbed, Elsie, but they are so soft,
Elsie, so soft, soft as your thighs, Elsie.

Cut.

The Ballad of the Pig Circus

I used to be stereotyped for my ambulance good looks
and a smile that says "I just stabbed my thigh with the
    sharp
end of a compass" like no other reference to the
    vaudeville era.
I used to tame dead horses and count cockroaches on
the gnarled arms of the downtown pretenders.
Then came the angel.

It woke me up one night poking me with a rifle
to check if I was sleeping or imitating its dead cousin.

I was imitating its dead cousin.
I was powerful as only a spoiled child can be.
The angel was spoiled as only meat can be.

It taught me to rifle through the faces of faceless
    victims.
But it was the Year of the Scab
and there was no room for people who act like
lawn fires when they should be modeling

I WRITE LIKE A GIRL,
YOU READ LIKE YOU'RE
IN THE CLOSET

the latest symptoms in remodeled scriptoriums.

That must be why the angel left me one night
and why I shattered its face
when I found it the next morning
taking a nap in the neighbor's baby crib.

I admit it wasn't the best solution,
but what do you expect from a Hollywood of dead
    horses?

The Second Cut of the Pig

The birth story of our nation is short. There was some
nature that needed to be cut. I hid silverware in the
tree. The first eyelids of our nation were taped open,
but then we shut them. Then we killed Indians. With
knives and forks. When we opened their bodies, we
didn't find any gold, just infected candy. Then we
orchestrated another genocide but we prefer Europe's
genocides because they're romantic, with the trains
and the silver teeth and they take your fur at the door.
Our genocides were far less artful. Someone who's
had to wash mucus and blood off the floor of a ship
is more likely to write an instructional booklet about
doll-collecting than to write a poem. We've made a
cold and very clammy doll in this tree. Yes, that's still
me up here but now I'm wearing the Mask of Reason.
Now I'm getting ready to jump down on your sister's
window ledge and sing her a sweete sweete melodye

about the loins, the fire and the dread, the charcoal
odor, the sting of gin. I'm putting on the Mask of
Treason. It itches.

Send in crackheads with clay feet
Send in tarp to cover up the sailors
Send in catatonics to cover up our television eyes
Send in archetypes of gravel
Send in grovelers and boasts
Send in fists on a silver plate
Send in cakewalks and cake shame and cake crowds
Send in the evidence of tampering
Send in the gravel empires
Send in raptures of feathers and fires
Send in laugh tracks
Send in tigers
Send in stranglers and ex girlfriends
Send in intruders and exploitation narratives
Send in pawnshop romances
Send in stalkers and forgivers
Send in breeders
Send in boom-boxes
Send in the sick sick song we sang
Send in the horselessness we sang about

Elsie your shadow Elsie your seal Elsie in my favorite
sitcom your behind sits in the milk bowl Elsie your
indie bands suck your tits I want to suck I want to
hurt your balloon but it's stuck in the telephone wire
stuck to my shoulders and its mouth can't say a word

that is not a shadow of your shapely body that is not
in English and about your big tits my milk sister my
little surgeon my tied-up deer my solved problem in
an abandoned vehicle.

Douse.

The Motif of the Fist in Vaudeville Shows

That theater is now a dog-training facility

I know I was there I bit and I chewed

I have a cuckoo in my trauerspiel

Melville is too busy jacking off in the customs house
to check the freight I'm bringing into the country.
His country is pale and the poachers need my bag of
orphans for their festivities. The festivities will take
place right here. No, right here, in my torso, my pig
roast, my oink-oink-you're-dead.

Elsie's balloon is so cute, it's a shame it's a condom.
It's a shame I have to use it for its true purpose – to
break.

I'm teaching a class on the ruin of aesthetics. My
class is full of girls wearing tiny athletic shorts and
tank tops. Their bodies are too well-nourished for the
history of hospitals, their faces are too round, smiling

for mass grave photography. Their eyes are too blue
to be fishes. In order for this class to change their
adorable little lives I must turn those pretty blue eyes
into codfish. I must catch them on my hook. I must
hang myself on the clothesline outside my childhood
house. The suburbs are made of cod skeletons hanging
on clotheslines. They jangle every time I fuck.

We built a hare throne of wonders
We used lye

I agree with Godard: In his movie about the Rolling
Stones the band appears so ridiculous in all their
artistry and re-takes compared to the spontaneous
beauty of juvenile delinquents spray-painting quotes
from Mao on a factory wall or the black militants
kidnapping the palest women in France. And yet here
I sit with my little devil inside some soundproof walls
trying the get the drums to be just right. I want them to
sound shattered as a doll's head.

I'm *so* 20th century.
I write poems about gasoline.
I paint the corridors in nail polish.
I love lips,
for they remind me that I'm alive and ticking
like a bomb in a schoolyard
or beneath a bed that hasn't been made

THE FIRST THING WE DO
IS GET RID OF
THE NATIVE SPEAKER

THE NEW EXHAUSTION

for almost 30 years now.
The bed is my left eye.
My right eye is the key
to the deserted circus animal.

(I wrote that poem a few months ago while working as
a landscaper in New York City.)

The Fable of the Pig

I'm revising the pig circus to include both the
Coca-Cola Cowboys with their religious machines
and the Queen Girl with her hundreds of strays
running through the streets at night. I'm erasing the
incriminating parts in which I plan to kill Elsie's new
boyfriend. How I plan to beat his face in, how I plan
to feed him ten pounds of his own flesh. Instead the
pig circus will be full of political satire. We'll have a
white house and amnesia. On the Fourth of July the
pigs will squeal. In the dirt the pope will try to get
away from the animals. Old men shouldn't wear such
white clothes in the dirt. Old men should hide their
ears when they're being trampled by pigs. Red. Old
men should wear red in the dirt. I'm even changing
the crowd. Instead of popcorn we'll have chicken
carcasses. That's why the queen and her hundred
strays will burst through the stands. There won't be
a queen. She'll be dogs. There won't be a crowd.
They'll be readers.

(Basquiat is painting my portrait but he's running out of rope.)

Our Lady of the Pig Circus

Everyone loses when the codfish jangles.

For Italo Calvino:
When visiting Athens, GA, don't forget to bring some berries to Necropolis. I love berries and so does my Egyptian dog. He loves my eyes too. He stays within striking distance. That's where the orphans come in, the orphans with their beautiful bright eyes glimmering in the dark.

Prayer from an Occupation:
This is my body. Drive out the pigeons and the moneylenders. Drive my stalking horse into the wilderness and abandon it, stitch by stitch. Burn down my father's market place for it's a house of mongering and anorexia. I've been counting the bullet holes in my proverbial brother to find out how much longer I must wait before I can return to the unadulterated elementary school from which I continue to pilfer my words. My proverbial brother has three more holes to go, one for each time I have bathed my Chinese daughter in nightmare seeds, one for each time I've desecrated my wilderness, one for my throbbing gazelle.

My proverbial brother is finished.

Send in the carpetbaggers.
Send in the armed idealists and freed slaves.

Their time is coming in my seashell.
Their time will be a cockfight, blindness.

Soak a pillow in vinegar.

Oration:
You're not a rider, said the reader to the insane asylum in Cairo. You're a spider, Elsie. But I came here through the desert on a gaggle horse, cried Peer Gynt into the breathalyzer. It don't matter whose clothes you wear, it's how you trap the vermin that counts, said the scientist into his microphone. Applause. When will they stop? Why do my students wear such skimpy outfits? Applause. I'm catching figurative rats in here! Applause. I love the mole just above your hip bone. Applause. Can I kiss that skin fold? Applause. Elise Beckman, why don't you answer? Applause. Have they stuffed your little mouth full of cake? Applause.

(Note to self: This exercise was not meant for people.)

The way you slipped out of your lovely little bikini as we made out in the salty water while the German tourists lazed around on the beach and my skull burned: Oink.

My bruises are nothing without you
My barnyard is nothing without
your smile. It doesn't even burn
And the horses escape.

"Rock n' Roll Host"

It's so bright in Necropolis the sunlight doesn't
even twitch. I've painted my Egyptian dog the color
of a burned-out Chevrolet as an attempt to teach
it devotion. I'm feeding it pig meat and making it
sniff your torn-up prom dress to teach it to track you
down in the woods. The problem is that it's too hot
in this high school mausoleum; the dog salivates and
this interferes with its sense of smell. This makes it
tick too loudly. It leads me out on gravel roads and
minimalist color fields. Now we're entering a stadium
full of white people singing songs about heartbreak
like they were ready to round up all the strays in town.
Maybe they'll take care of my dog. They won't need
subtitles.

You have taken everything dark in my road movie
and turned it into a corset.
You have taken a man you despise and turned him
into a cage. I know the animals you want to keep
in there. It's not broken enough.

We did the brilliant cuckoo with your hands tied
above your head. We did the angry cuckoo against he
wall. We did the cracked cuckoo on glass. We did the

AFTER PERFORATION, MORE PERFORATION

leaky cuckoo. We did the sweet cuckoo. We wanted
to push the gates open for the cuckoo but now the
cuckoo is pecking at my skin. It wants back. Applause.

Bare Ruined Choir

The gypsy told me I was a ruined pilgrim, I would
never amount to anything more exact than jungle or
asphalt. Applause.

Elsie,
If you ever marry, Talking Heads will reunite
and play "Burning Down the House" at your reception.
I will reunite and play gravel roads with my hands
and your immortal sister.
You will probably hula-hoop on the stage.
You know how I love it when you hula hoop.
Especially when you're just wearing
your pink underwear with little flowers.

Applause.

The False Wedding of Elsie Beckman – A Lurid Case
  History

When Elsie Beckman returned from the junkyard she
abandoned all my love poems in a '65 Plymouth. She
was a few years older, a few pounds heavier, but now
she "loved" her body and felt comfortable going to the

beach in a baby-blue bikini which was a wonderful size too small. She married the boy she told me was "pretty ugly, boring and incredibly materialistic" because he was "the opposite of you, dependable, doesn't fight back." Do you want to know what happened to me after the junkyard was over? I joined the Fascist Party like my grandparents and spent the rest of my life stabbing the pillow where her head used to be.

Today I noticed a strand of her hair I hadn't seen before.

Applause.

The best kind of beauty is leaky.
The best kind of hole is the beginning of a story.
The best kind of blossom is hardening in my head.
The best kind of architecture is dorms.

The Whoroscope

The girls in this town are well-nourished and tan. I'm watching one in a café on College Road. She has beautiful bare shoulders and she's wearing a tight black tank top. There are vague highlights in her brown hair. She's reading the classified section. I wonder if I'm in her classified section? I know I'm in the whoroscope. It says: "Johannes, look to your right! There's a girl with pigtails! Johannes, there are pictures of heroes on the walls! Johannes, you

will never be able to keep Candy safe. Johannes, you
will never be able to keep Candy locked in your safe
because, Johannes, your safe is not safe. It's an organ.
Johannes, you're the monkey."

(The silver fever I hustle
isn't meant as a love song for you.
It's meant to explain religion
to demonstrate the significance
of imperialism,
to pig at your thighs.)

DEAR PRESIDENT WITH BLEACHERS

Your daughter looked unbreakable at first. Her eyes were closed while I picked the splinters out of her rocking horse. The scariest part about that horse is the religious implications of infanticide. The scariest part about the raided warehouse is your daughter's erratic breathing. Your daughter and I built this strychnine paradise. Now we have to stab our bed in it. Now I want to wash your daughter's hair in turpentine. I must look provisional now as I sit in this stale chair your daughter and I built with our hands last night. Your daughter and I must look carsick.

Stop talking.

No, not you – the boy carrying a lamb across the dance floor. He doesn't understand why I want to listen to your daughter's damaged bird breaths when there is all this bleating in which I could indulge. I caught that boy playing family with himself last night. You played the Great White Father in Washington with great stamina and style. Your daughter covered you in wool. I didn't even recognize you when you chased her through the iconoclastic riot.

I didn't believe you when you said
Berlin was part of her body,
a dangerous maybe even shameless part
that would lead me to paranoia or the opera.

Since the dawn of time daughters have wanted to slit their fathers' throats with their boyfriends' knives.

Since the beginning of this poem I have tried to lie
about your daughter, insinuating that she's mine, that
we fucked behind the football bleachers one chilly
autumn night and gave our children off-putting names
like "Hiroshima" and "You Weren't There, You Didn't
See Anything" to evoke the heart-attack clamor of
European cinema.

The truth is your daughter is nearly impossible to
    catch.
She's quick in the night as LA is bright
when it's burning to the ground.
You need torch-lit charades. You need marching boots.
You need pliers. You need a new thorn to
jam into your thigh. You need me and my plague
    diction
if you ever hope to pick your daughter out of this
    quarantine.

Your daughter has drops of sweat tattooed on the
inside of her thighs. She calls them "my little birdies."
Calls me her "private metaphysical joke" when
we're drunk in her room and the stereo is blasting
dance music. Calls me "derivative" when she hasn't
taken her medicine. Calls this island "Throbbing." I
trust the pet-trainers. They call it "Hide-and-Seek."
Astronomers call it "The Body," but they're even
more paranoid than I am.

The only thing I'm bringing with me when I leave this
island is a pack of cards to tell my future and a pack of

dogs to tell my past. My favorite card has nosebleed in a black garbage bag. I think that means a career in politics but the deck was designed by a pedophile and I always fail to take that into account when I read my fortune in a throaty voice. The cards look funny when I see them as my future, but less promising when I notice the studies of infant anatomy in the truck wheels.

This part of the poem is called "The Swimming Pool," even though I don't have chlorine in my eyes, even though it's actually called "Rise" after my favorite palace song about police brutality.

The next part of this poem is also called "Rise." I love this song – scrambled lyrics, dirt road, open windows, cold arms, cigarette smoke. It's about a girl who thinks she's a drive-by shooting and a boy who belongs to a vanishing act. Lets see if they can make it out of there. Lets see if they can sterilize the binoculars. Lets see about the rope. The chicken. Lets kiss with our mouths open. Lets see if the boy can keep the girl safe. If he can break the ice with his bicycle. If the fish will keep them warm. Lets see which one can breath through the plastic. The mask has tears for eyes and no mouth. It looks like salvation. Lets see if it is. Lets see what kind of house they build with this deck of cards. No, don't tell me that. I'm scared of houses.

I WILL CARVE LIKE
YOU'RE ON FIRE

I was born in an evacuation drill, but that's no excuse.
I want my own mauled place in the sun, but my eyes
feel feathery and the claptraps I arrive in are always
raw. The girls fall off their bicycles. The minstrel
show doesn't sound enough like a lynching and the
subway car squeals and bangs with pigs. The actor
who plays Zeitgeist with the neighbors' little girl used
to work in a chicken factory. I used to work like a fist
but now I work until lye burns my fingers.

Explanation for cutters: Use the sharp end of the
   compass.
Explanation for stick-figure experts: If you can't steal
   any pigs, use my thighs.

Use my thighs. I'm graduating from the school of skin
flicks. I need some bamboo huts to shoot some natives
in. I need. I need. The woman I love leaves the Night
of Long Knives to the lambs and laughs on my chest
as if we were already out of the gothic tale I've been
beating with a hammer since 1991. I've finished my
love affair with freezing water. It ends with a binge.
The faculty calls me "the rioted one," even though I
know how to use a hose.

I can hardly hear my torso for the static.
I collected the horse skeleton on a beach.
I should get the rabies out of my eyes.

Never mind my neck. I've already sold it to the
highest bidder, a necklace manufacturer from World

War II. I will wear it to your graduation from shotgun primitivism. Now we can all watch you improvise in the kill shelter. The camera crew is suffering from a skin disorder. It's almost dawn. It's a slammed door. We're alone in the guest room.

I hope you brought the props.

When discussing the phenomenon of the circus that no longer runs away, it's important to touch on the beauty of mass graves. My crew still thinks this poem is about a soccer stadium. The girls are getting cold in the parking lot. Look at them shivering on the cement. Somebody bring that one a blanket.

When discussing my slurred coronations it's important to pay attention to wasps and needles. The thinner leaves a glow on the canvas. The dancers can't figure out how to carve "salvation" in the canvas when the pigs twitch uncontrollably. The style is figurative. The squeals are ideal.

Explanation for insect collectors: My revival stories
    aren't true.

For one, my body isn't locked in my sweetheart's cabinet. Secondly, she's not my sweetheart. She's my sweat-heart at the cakewalk arranged in honor of the latest gag order. Most importantly, I won't hurt anybody's pet broken arm, not even the shovel I've

BLACKFACE IS NOT ENOUGH

been using so forcefully.

Yes, I spend words the way a homeless man
spends money on pedicures for prostitutes
who barely let him finger them.

If I didn't have such perfect nails, would you still hum
along? Would you use a hammer? Will this night end
on a wrist-cracked note? Please end. Please now. The
horse skeleton is raided. The basement is blatant. The
police heard I spent hours at a children's cancer ward
interviewing the nurses about God. I found out about
gravity from fucking an eye doctor in Harlem. The
symbolism was redundant. The racism was a jacket
full of swans. They're bursting out.

Next unit: White Out

snow
porcelain
sheets
women
fence
skin
crash
cake
house
lips
powder
elections

Minority stereotypes running around Central Park
with bricks and other clichés: Get out your umbrella
definitions. The party has started in our indecipherable
homeland.

Next unit: Open.

Ground zero for figurative language: heat symbols are
natural while cars are crashing the classroom full of
ribs. Only two or three cracked on impact. Only the
women can't speak anymore because I've stuffed their
holes. Their mouths are open. They can't close them.
That's what the night is for, crawling in on all fours,
all eights, all horse legs, all spasms on this side of the
railroad tracks.

Don't knock.
We can't let you out
of the blurred costume
until it's too dark
to find your whistle
beneath all this debris.

The plastic bottle is pierced by a fence post.
The bird heart is pierced by a safety pin.

Please, Melee, just because you are my sister doesn't
mean I can't shake like a tree that will burn in the
next children's crusade. Please, jackal-hearted masses,
erect a statue to commemorate the red hands of

the thieves that taught me everything I know about
tenderness. Please, Hypothermia.

SCRAPE GRACE

My wife has emptied the chest. Outside: trees teem
with birds. You won't find a single feather in here.
My torso is clean. My wife is hammering. Ribs
echo a slurred horse skeleton. I'm taking advantage
of the money involved in dried meats. My wife is
pedaling the last of my collection of smiles. Here is
a child star tied up in my basement. Here is me and
birds on a beach in southern France. Here is a fuzzy
photograph my wife took while there was something
at stake in the struggle against the state. Here is me
impersonating the state with a stuffed parrot on my
back and my feet on a parrot coming undone in the
snow. That's stuffing. That's snow. That's my hand.

How to Build Your Wife a Mute Cabinet:

When prying the nails out of a chest
don't use the hammer (unless you've given up).
When picking the knickknack out
of a chest be sure not to forget to pick
the cartilage off the chicken carcass.
There are many ways a chest can go wrong.
When the chest is finished
get started on the birds they are so colorful
in flight when they sing they are so
flavorful when grilled they are morning
they are organs they breathe in my room
on the third floor of the House of Reason.
I started to have a problem
with their cackling, their lack of hygiene.
I had to call the exterminator my riot
before she agreed to turn the sound off.

My wife, the Marvellian, knows how to pluck feathers out of my eyes. She doesn't need a hammer to take an X-ray photograph of my chest, but that works better than a drill. I don't need a shell but I keep whispering into her folds. I tell them about salt and ocean and driftwood, but I have trouble speaking with all these rocks inside my mouth.

Where is my wife? Who is she talking to? She should be here cleaning out the chest that has grown cold on us again. A clammy chest is no good in the equestrian anatomies of afternoon, the stricken neighs.

The Story of Origins Begins Here:
We have finally come to the mythology we came here
    to fuck up.
My body fucked eight times in the last 12 hours. Its
    husk makes no sound.

Interlude:
It suddenly occurs to me that I dreamed this poem last night. Last night in my dream my wife said, "Don't use a cliché like parrot in a poem about my sex drive." Last night she showed me her poem, a little piece of wood with two small metal pieces nailed into it. "It was built by a little man from Luleå," she explained.

Interlude:
The cage is colorful and well-decorated like a Catholic myth about car accidents. I might say the cage is

teeming with mythologies but my wife is in the next
room writing a poem about that precise matter. She's
a practical woman. She plans to hawk this poem as an
instruction manual.

We're coming to a town near you:
My wife will drive. I'm an opera that way. We
talk about the New Critics as if they were interior
decorators, as if they could clean a chest out with a
dull blade. I use a tuning fork. That's how I entertain
my wife.

(And yet the little man from Luleå cut her a piece
of wood. When I looked at it I had to scream until
my lungs were empty. That was the scary part of the
dream, the part that reminded me of childhood, the
part I never told my wife about.)

Basilisk in the Beauty Mirror
(Some Necessary Autobiographical Details):

I was born.
Rudely plucked, I became
a berry-picking man, flushed and boggy
beneath the lashes of the sun,
rummaging on the banks of the rough
river rubbing the hard land.
The sun was aghast on my shoulders.
Someone followed us back from
the grave-robbery. Her feet were
mothy, her breath sour.

Considering the overwhelming historical precedents, it may surprise you: I turned around.

POSTCARDS

Dear Abbey,
I'm covered with snow.
I'm covered with snow.
And it's laying its eggs
in the most embarrassing
parts of my body.

Dear Natalie,
To take some sleeping pills
and crawl back
into bed with you.

Dear Amanda,
You don't want to die in a city where you can't even
live, wrote the German poet who was killed by a car.
I could die in this city if a big truck plowed into me.
My shoulders would buckle and my breastcage would
break.

Dear Amy,
Sometimes I think I was a truck in another lifetime—a truck parked on a county road next to a field full of dried scraps of corn. And if you look in the back of it you may think it belongs to a lover because of the broken glass, or a barber because of the shears, or a fool because the letters are torn, or a child because the guns are not loaded. Sometimes I think I was a truck that smashed a ribcage. Sometimes I think I was the ribcage.

Dear Mr. Springsteen,
My truck keeps driving off bridges. The animals inside the truck drown. When they haven't called for a few days their parents get nervous and start calling the glue factory. They're worried that their children have thrown away their educations and followed my path - trying to keep things together that should fall apart or trying to stick things together that don't belong together. The parents understand that it's better to burn such garbage or even recycle it and turn it into black rulers for school children who'll grow up to fuck someone they hate in a public bathroom or try to smash their heads against the wall or eat pot because they can't find a goddamned pipe or go skipping down the avenue of asses. That's the life the animals will never know. I'm trying to tell them there's no point in struggling. My truck is stuck on the bottom of the river and nobody has a submarine that goes this far beneath the skin.

Dear Screen Door,
You're a true joker in a city full of people who hurt me when they try to smile. I have noticed how you imitate my days by standing still. I've seen you imitate my ways by slamming in the wind. I hear you imitate my laughter when I'm trying hard to fall asleep.

Dear Mom,
I thought I was in love, but then I found out it was bipolar disorder.
Don't ask me how I feel. Put out that cigarette on your thigh.

Dear Dad,
I'm fine.

Dear Lovely Sunday Morning Coming Down,
I will always remember your porno and your cold
 coffee.
I will always remember your floor and your birdcage.

THE LAST INSTRUMENT

The speed of horses. The steel of cars. The black of flash. The glass of hands. The steam of skin. The scar of lips. The dance of blights. The neighs of teeth. The road of sand. The road of run. The road of raw. The wheels of stars. The crash of hair. The kiss of stares. The breast of blue. The pluck of screws. The little little space between very and large. The little little race run from here to there. The bare snare growing out of the clothes. The hooves the skin the dance the dance of blights. That's how you learn how to play the instrument you wear around your neck. You have seven seconds.

I remembered how I had seen Johannes the time I tried to return to the house after we had been exchanged: he had been shut into the entrance hall. He stood on the other side of the glass window and was not allowed to speak to me, and he scraped his nail against the glass window as if he wanted to put an invisible mark on it. And I thought that he was like a bird there behind the window, a bird that touched it with the tips of his wings, because that is how muted his heavy breaths were, and how hidden his tears, that I could only hear the sound of his nail against the window, like a bird's wing-tips against the window that shut him out from the freedom that I suddenly understood was me."

A NEW QUARANTINE WILL TAKE MY PLACE

The paper lantern is as quiet as a mouse now, as quiet as a heap of mice crawling on each other trying to eat their way out of a trashcan. The sound of paper crinkling suggests there is something unsanitary about this Easter. The squeaking is emblematic of our superstitions. Our science is quiet as the mice we have cut open to conduct tests on in laboratories and cinematic suburbs. The suburbs are as quiet as a plastic bag whispering on a child's head. Empty candy wrappers are falling out of my pillow. The voice works like the police force in this blackmail trial of an afternoon. The voice can't be a window unless it bloats light.

The window is empty with blotched sky and trees look so much thinner when you are a landscape painter than when you are a kleptomaniac. On this island everything I say sounds ekphrastic. I'm doing my best imitation of an echo in this wheelbarrow: I chew on beef jerky. I try to understand why the human beings here have been filled in with markets, why the birth document is incomplete.

My joy is in my red paper lantern and it's spilling light. The white walls are undulating. My joy is a frozen hare in hard air.

The butcher shop has nothing on my joy. I own the kind of joy that is impossible to stitch into a wedding dress, to blare like gashes, to dig a tunnel, to flood afternoon.

Still Life in a Glass House with Ritalin and Snow

The taxidermist has become a beloved representative
of all that is lovely about accents. Adaptation has
become an auction barker. Up next: My joy! The jack-
o-lantern is being used to shoot deer in the woods.
Dry leaves crackle in my feet. I just need to make it
to the end of the week before letting the hoards out of
the display case. Without the museum I know nothing
about lingerie or stampedes, but I can't live in here if I
can't tame the pale blotching up my window.

In exile literature, dead bees inside the window have
    become a trope
demonstrating the influence of Jewish folklore.
In exile literature, there is much running, much
    sunburn,
much necking and many parodic bestiaries.
My exile literature of this island is populated with
    side-stitches.

In theory, the silk route of my joy should not be hard
to unravel. I have a mouth like any other forger of
official denouements. I have built a New Jerusalem
based on my experiences in an abortion clinic. My
main model was the shipwreck of a birthday ditty.
My model wore a blurred gown and a salty mouth I
wanted to retain in spite of all the rapping on her door.
The new life had to be postponed. The blush light
danked.

I have learned everything I know about peepholes
   from rattlesnakes.
I have learned about eyes from flag-burnings.

   I keep a gloat of birds in my breathing.

The first arena of visibility will be the locusts
descending on the island. The second vision will
be the eye of a locust as it sits on the edge of my
trashcan. I can already imagine the rustle of candy
wrappers as the stitches come out as I come out
of the bric-a-brac. It is wonderful to scrape such a
naturalistic frenzy on one's own sheets. It's even
more wonderful to languish in a pillow hiatus while
the tigers and lions fight. I've gathered these mute
moments in my language lessons. I want to populate
your daughter with squirrels.

The language that is spoken in my ear sounds more
like candy wrappers than Moses' wrist lectures, more
like fish-squirms than Florida. The natives were
brought to this island like a fashion travesty.

The precedent for my kind of homesickness is the
longing of German mercenaries. They were treated
with leaches. I'm treating you tenderly for fear that
you will tear down my posters, my elaborate life
work of anatomical research of wedding dresses, fish
songs, citation disorders. Don't wreck the bestiary
until I have traced the introduction of trick birds to
this island. This delinquency is like noises, sounds and

sweet airs. My baby's skin is like a door.

Hello, don't you recognize my jewelry.

I want to come back into my snake-handling. I want to open a lingerie store to sell some portraits of drowning victims. I want to restore the church where the inmates were born ornate with strings and ceiling tendrils. I want to tug my baby into the blaretorium where I learned this extinct style from the artisans who had been used as corruption allegories in their boggy youths. Welcome to my corruption.

Welcome to my new corner of a hundred years.

Snow clumps. Branches bramble. Dead leaves look like strips of yellowed newspaper. Afternoon: Congested.

The wall makes my ear cold. The train is throbbing close. It will take me to the horizon.

Even as my broken windows and hairless mice run out of significance in the island vocabulary, I feel a further frenzy. Even a surgeon knows no such stitches.

Some of the poems in this manuscript have previously appeared in the following journals: *American Letters & Commentary, Canary, Gulf Coast, Hotel America, jubilat, Jacket, Octopus, n/or, Salt Hill, Verse* and *Black Clock*, as well as in the anthologies *Free Radicals* (Subpress, 2003) and *PP/FF: An Anthology* (Starcherone Books, 2006).

The quote on page 124 is from P.O. Enquist's Kapten *Nemos Bibliotek* (my translation).

"We Will Use Clothes-Hangers Next Time" was arranged by Lara Glenum.